PURNELL LITTLE READERS

Titles in this series:

The Magic Lemonade
The Six Fairy Dolls
The Runaway Cheeses
The Pixie in the Pond
The Dog With the Long Tail
The Bear With Boot-Button Eyes
The Little Sugar Mouse
Dame Roundy's Stockings
The Good Old Rocking Horse
The Goblin and the Dragon

Enid Blyton's

The Magic Lemonade
and other stories

Enid Blyton's

The Magic Lemonade

and other stories

PURNELL

SBN 361 03462 8

Published 1976 by Purnell Books, Berkshire House,
Queen Street, Maidenhead, Berkshire
Made and printed in Great Britain by Purnell and Sons Limited,
Paulton (Avon) and London

CONTENTS

The Magic Lemonade

Charlie Brown was a very horrid little boy. He used to tease all the animals he met, chop worms in half, tread on beetles, and take birds' eggs from their nests. No cat liked him, and every dog in his village used to bark at him as he went by. He really was a most unpleasant little boy.

But one day he had his punishment, and it happened like this. He was going through the woods on a very hot day, throwing his cap at every butterfly he saw, when he suddenly felt very thirsty.

"Oh, my!" said Charlie. "If only I could see a ginger-beer shop, I'd spend five pence on a lovely drink. Oh, I am thirsty!"

Now just as he said that he came to a little table under a tree. By it was a chair, and on the table was a jug of lovely green-yellow lemonade. There was a glass there, too, and Charlie stopped and looked at it for a long time.

Nobody was about at all. Charlie looked this way and that, but there wasn't anyone in sight. Then at last the sight of that jug of lemonade was too much for him. He ran up to the table, sat down on the chair, and poured himself out a full glass. He drank it without stopping once to take breath and then he poured out another glass.

It was the nicest lemonade he had ever tasted. Charlie drank the second glassful, and poured himself out a third. He emptied the glass again, and set it down on the table with a sigh. He wasn't thirsty any more.

Just as he was going to get up and go on his way again, a small man came running up. He stopped in surprise when he saw Charlie.

"What do you mean by drinking all my lemonade?" he asked, sternly.

"I was thirsty," said Charlie. "I couldn't help it."

"Well, it was magic lemonade," said the little man. "You'll be very sorry you drank it, soon."

"You're only saying that to frighten me," said Charlie. "I don't believe it!"

He marched off through the woods, whistling. He didn't believe a word that the little man had said. But all the same the lemonade was magic! It had the power of making a boy or girl become very small indeed, but Charlie didn't know that.

Now, as he went along, he suddenly saw a robin's nest built in an old saucepan on the ground. It had four tiny birds in it, and Charlie thought it would be funny to take them out of the nest and see what the mother bird did when she came back. So he lifted the little things out one by one – and just as he was doing that the magic lemonade very suddenly began to work. He grew rapidly smaller, and it was a very queer feeling – just as if he had gone down in a very fast lift and come to the bottom with a bump. He shut his eyes and gasped.

When he opened them again he was very small indeed – smaller than the smallest of the baby birds he had taken from the nest. He couldn't make it out at all. The grass around him was above his head, and the nest in the saucepan seemed enormous. The little birds near were as big as ostriches to him, and he felt quite afraid of them.

Suddenly the mother bird swooped down, and saw her little ones out of the cosy nest.

"Twit-it-it!" she scolded. "Who has done this? Why, here is that horrid boy again, and he has grown very small! It must have been he who did this. You nasty little boy, I shall peck you!"

She flew at the frightened boy and pecked him on the arm. Her beak tore a large hole in his sleeve, and he was very much frightened. He turned away and ran for his life. The robin flew after him, and gave him another hard peck that pulled his jersey in half. He began to cry.

"Ha, how do you like being ill-treated?" cried the robin. "Isn't it nice? Don't you enjoy it? Here's another peck for you!"

But the third peck missed Charlie, for he had seen a big worm-hole and down it he ran full-speed. It was very dark at first, but soon he was able to see the narrow, winding passage. He walked on down it, wondering where it led to, and hoping that it would take him above ground again soon.

At last he came to a wider part where a kind of little room was hollowed out. In it was a coiled-up worm who poked out his head as soon as he heard Charlie coming.

"Oh, I thought you were a mole after me," he said. "What are you doing down here, and what is your name?"

"I am Charlie Brown and I have escaped from a robin that pecked me," said Charlie.

"What!" cried the worm. "You are that horrid, nasty Charlie! Why, you killed my brother yesterday by chopping him in half, do you know that? What did you do it for?"

"I-I-I-I don't know," said Charlie. "I'm very s-s-s-sorry."

"That won't help my poor brother worm," said the worm, angrily. "I think I'll chop you in half, then you'll know what it is like."

He uncoiled himself and looked about, and Charlie was afraid that he was going to find a chopper. He didn't wait another minute but took to his heels and fled along the burrow once more. It led him upwards again at last, and the little boy put his head out of the hole to see if all was safe.

He could see and hear nothing of the robin, so he walked quietly out of the hole.

"I think I'd better try to go home," he thought. "Mummy will know me, even if I am very tiny, and perhaps she can give me some medicine to make me grow big again."

So he tried to find the path that led to his home – but it was very difficult because the grass seemed like trees to him, and as for the trees themselves, why, it took him quite ten minutes to walk round the trunk of even one of them!

Suddenly he heard the flutter of wings and looked up. Above him he saw a great butterfly, which seemed as big as an aeroplane to him. It was all colours and very beautiful – but one of its wings was torn.

"Ho!" it cried in a loud, shrill voice. "What's this funny little creature? Why, I do believe it's that horrid boy who threw his cap at me a little while ago and spoilt one of my lovely wings. He's gone small! Now's the time to pay him back for his cruelty!"

He swooped down at Charlie, and hit him with one of his big wings. The little boy felt as if someone had slapped him hard, and once more he began to run. The butterfly flew after him and gave him such a hard smack that Charlie fell over on his face. He rolled under a dandelion leaf and the butterfly couldn't see him.

Charlie lay there quite still, hoping that the butterfly would go away. When he peeped out he

saw it far away in the distance, so he crept out and dusted his clothes.

"Oh, I do wish I hadn't been unkind to so many things!" he thought. "It's going to be very difficult to get home because I may meet lots more things that want to pay me back for teasing them."

He set off once more, and this time he ran into a bright-copper beetle, nearly as big as himself.

"Look where you're going," said the beetle, sharply.

"The same to you!" said Charlie, rudely.

"I seem to know that cheeky voice," said the beetle, looking at Charlie thoughtfully. "Yes! Dear me, it's the nasty little boy who trod on my cousin this morning! What has made you so small?"

Charlie wished he hadn't been rude to the beetle. He made no answer and tried to creep away behind a daisy. But the beetle was much too quick. He put out his front leg and caught hold of the little boy tightly. Charlie wriggled and got away—but no sooner had he dodged round the daisy than he felt himself tightly nipped by the arm, and to his dismay he found that an earwig had got him in its nippers.

"Here you are, Beetle!" cried the earwig. "I've got him for you!"

The beetle came running up, and laughed to see Charlie so firmly caught.

"It's Charlie Brown," he said to the earwig. "Have you heard of him?"

"Of course!" said the earwig, nipping Charlie

playfully on the right ear. "He stamped on my whole family last week, and I was the only one that escaped. Oh, I know this boy very well indeed."

He nipped Charlie on the other ear and the little boy began to cry.

"What shall we do with him?" asked the earwig.

He let go Charlie's arm for half a second to wave his nippers at the butterfly who was flying up once more. Charlie took his chance and fled off as fast as he could with all the others after him. He came to a foxglove and climbed hurriedly up the stem. Then he crawled into one of the flowers and lay there hardly daring to breathe.

He saw the others go quickly by without seeing him, and he was very glad. He was just going to crawl out of the foxglove when he heard a tremendous booming sound near him, and an enormous bumble-bee appeared at the mouth of the flower. He stared in surprise to see Charlie.

"What are you doing here?" he asked. "I didn't know that little boys got honey from flowers."

"I was only hiding," said Charlie.

"What are you hiding for?" asked the bee. "Have you done something wrong?"

Charlie didn't answer, and the bee scratched his head and looked at him.

"I do believe you're Charlie Brown," he said at last. "You're very much smaller than when I last saw you, but all the same I think I'm right. You threw a stone at a blackbird, and it missed it and hit me instead, almost breaking my wings. Yes, I'm sure you're Charlie Brown. I think I'll sting you. That will teach you not to be unkind to other creatures."

"Oh, please, please, don't!" cried Charlie, in fright.

"On second thoughts I won't waste my nice barbed sting on you," said the bee. "I'll fetch my friend the wasp and he can sting you instead. Ho, ladybird, come here! Watch and see that this boy doesn't get out of the foxglove till I come back."

The ladybird flew up and perched on the edge of the flowers. She knew Charlie quite well, for he had tried to catch her the week before. The bee flew off with a zooming sound, and Charlie trem-

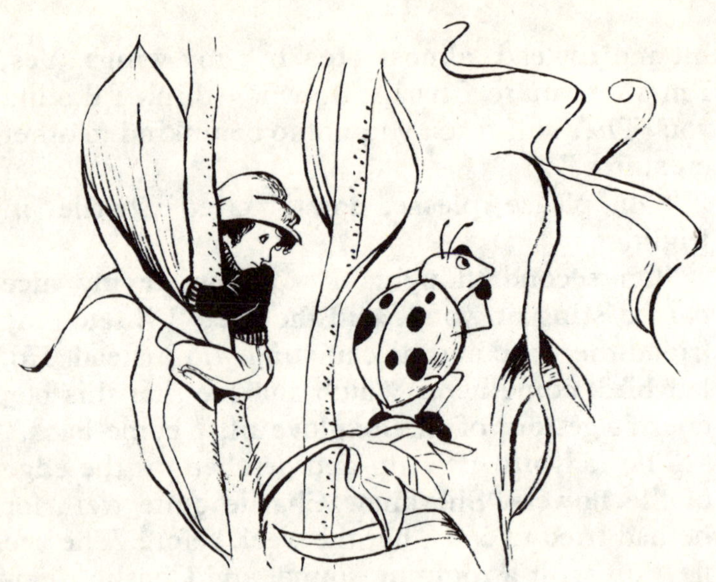

bled to think of the wasp coming to sting him.

Suddenly an ant down below called out to the ladybird: "Ladybird, ladybird, fly away home, your home is all burnt and your children are gone!"

"Oh, dear, dear!" cried the ladybird. "I must hurry away. Stay here, boy, till the bee comes back, or he will be very cross with me."

As soon as the ladybird had spread her wings and flown away, Charlie crept quickly out of the foxglove, slid down the stalk and ran off through the tall grass as fast as he could go. He heard a buzzing, droning sound overhead and dived under a buttercup leaf. He peeped out and saw the bumble-bee flying with a wasp, and went quite pale to think what might have happened to him if he had still been in the foxglove.

Soon he went on again, keeping a very careful look-out. After he had wandered for a long time, trying in vain to find the right path, he heard a great noise of voices. He crept behind a nettle and peeped to see what was going on.

Sitting in a grassy ring were many birds, butterflies and insects. Two dogs were there, and a cat. Also a hedgehog and a little red squirrel.

And they were all talking about Charlie! The news had soon got round that he had become smaller than any of them, and they had all met to discuss how they should find him and punish him for his unkindness to them!

"I'll go one way," said the cat, "and the dogs can go another. The butterflies can fly all about and look into each flower to see if he's there. The beetles can . . ."

But Charlie didn't wait to hear any more. He ran for his life! And alas for him! He didn't look where he was going and he fell straight into a sticky spider's web! He struggled and struggled to free himself, but it was no use. He was caught far too tightly.

In a trice a great spider ran out to the middle of her web and stared at the little boy.

"You're a funny sort of fly!" she said. "I've never seen your kind before. What are you?"

"I'm not a fly!" said Charlie. "I'm a little boy. Please, please, let me go!"

"A little boy!" said the spider. "Now I wonder if you can be Charlie Brown? I made a web in his

garden one day and he broke it all to bits. Then I made another and he broke that one too. Then I made a third, a really beautiful one, and he destroyed that one too. So I came here to the woods, where I have been happy ever since."

Charlie was very much frightened to hear the spider say all this. He tried his hardest to break out of the web, but it held him fast.

"Yes, you are Charlie Brown," said the spider. "There's a reward out for you, you know. All the birds and animals are looking for you. I shall take you to them, and get the reward!"

The spider tied Charlie up with some web, and carried him off to the grassy ring where all the animals were. They were still talking, and when the spider appeared with Charlie they looked very much astonished.

"Here he is! Here he is!" they cried. "Now we've got him! The spider's caught him! What shall we do with him?"

"Smack him!" cried the butterflies.

"Bite him!" cried the dogs.

"Scratch him!" cried the cat.

"Pinch him!" cried the earwigs.

"Tread on him!" cried the beetles.

"No, no!" cried Charlie. "Please forgive me. I'll never be unkind again."

"Can anyone say a good word for him?" asked the cat. There was a great silence. Charlie looked round hoping that one of the company there could say at least one good word for him, but not a single word was said.

"No one says anything for you," said the cat, sternly. "So I am afraid you must be well punished."

"There's just one thing that ought to be said," cried the squirrel, coming forward. "He has a dear little sister, who loves every bird and animal there is. She loves this nasty little boy too, and it would make her very unhappy if we bit him and scratched him, pecked him and pinched him."

"Alice Brown nursed me when I broke my leg in a trap," said a sandy rabbit.

"Alice Brown fed my little ones when they fell out of the nest," said a big blackbird.

"Alice Brown put out nuts for me to eat last autumn," said the squirrel.

"Alice Brown said she was very sorry when she accidentally trod on the end of my tail," said a worm.

"Alice Brown gave me crumbs all last winter," said the robin.

"Good gracious me!" said the cat. "Fancy such a horrid boy having such a nice sister! Does she really love him, do you think?"

"Oh, yes," said the dog. "I've seen her giving him all her chocolate, and doing his homework for him, and comforting him when he's been sent to bed for being naughty. She really does love him, and it would make her very unhappy if we punished Charlie too much."

"What shall we do, then?" asked everyone.

Then Charlie opened his mouth and spoke in a very small voice.

"If you would all forgive me, and give me just one more chance, I would never be nasty or horrid to any of you again. I didn't know before how frightening it was to be hunted and nipped and chased."

The creatures all looked at one another.

"Shall we forgive him or not?" asked the cat. "Shall we give him one more chance?"

"YES!" cried all the animals, birds, and insects in a loud voice. "Give him another chance, and let him go."

The spider came forward to undo the web that bound Charlie up so tightly—and just at that moment a queer thing happened. The magic in the lemonade stopped working, and Charlie suddenly shot up to his own height again, and became a proper little boy, far bigger than cats or dogs, beetles or birds.

The animals watched in surprise, too astonished to run away. What would Charlie do now that he was bigger and stronger than they were? Would he forget his promise and begin to hurt them again?

"Don't be afraid of me," said the little boy, when he had got back his breath again. "I won't hurt you, even though I am bigger than you now. I will always keep my word and be kind. I will never forget that you gave me one more chance."

"Hurrah!" shouted the dogs, and they frisked up to Charlie and licked his hand. "He's going to be just as nice as Alice!"

Charlie ran home. He found Alice and told her all that had happened.

"I may not remember to be always kind at first," he said, "so do please help me, Alice. I want to keep my promise because it was so nice of them all to give me another chance. If it hadn't been for you, I think they would have punished me dreadfully."

"I'll help you," said Alice, and she did. And now there isn't a pin to choose between them, for two nicer children you couldn't wish to meet!

The Boy Who Ran Away

There was once a little boy called Alec, who was always running away from things.

He ran away if he saw a dog coming. He ran out of any field that had cows in it. He ran away from bigger boys. He ran away and hid when a storm came. He was a dreadful runner-away.

His mother tried to stop him from always running away. "You mustn't be a little coward!" she said. "Stand up to things, and you'll find that nothing horrid will happen to you! The dogs won't bite you. The cows won't hurt you. The big boys won't hit you. The storm won't eat you!"

But it wasn't a bit of good – poor old Alec kept running away. He could run very fast, too!

Now one day his mother sent him out shopping. She gave him a shopping list to take with him. Alec read it out to himself as he trotted off to the shops, keeping a good look-out for dogs and cows.

"Butter, eggs, bacon, cakes, lard, flour, jam – my, what a lot of things!" he thought. "I can get them all at the grocer's."

He met no dogs, except a puppy who ran away from him. Alec didn't run away because you really can't run from things that run away from you. He met no cows, and not even a horse. He only saw one child, and that was a girl smaller than himself, so he was quite happy.

He went to the grocer's. There were a lot of people waiting to be served. One of them was a big boy. Alec thought he looked rather rough and untidy. He kept to the other side of the shop, because he didn't like rough and untidy boys. They had a habit of saying something rude and putting out their tongues – and that kind of thing made Alec afraid.

"Give me your basket, little fellow, and I'll put all the things into it," said the busy grocer's wife. "Is this your mother's list? All right, just wait here a few minutes and I'll hand you back your basket with everything in it."

The grocer was serving the big boy. The big boy stared at Alec. Alec turned away and began to look at a picture on a biscuit tin.

"Oh, here's my bad little dog come to find me!" suddenly said the big boy. "You rascal! Didn't I put you into your kennel and lock you up so that you couldn't run after me and worry everybody with your naughty ways! Go home, sir, go home!"

The dog was a big puppy. He gambolled round the big boy, and Alec went into a corner. He was afraid of the big puppy. The big boy took the puppy firmly by the collar and led him to the door.

OSED

"Go home, sir!" he said. Alec wondered if he could slip out of the other door of the shop before the puppy came back again, and before the big boy stared at him any more. He caught up the basket and ran out at top speed!

He tore down the road, swinging the basket in his hand. Then, to his horror, he heard the big boy shouting after him.

"Hi, you! Come back!"

Alec turned and saw the big boy running out of the shop, basket in hand, puppy at his heels. But Alec didn't stop. Oh, no – he ran on faster than ever!

"Hi, COME BACK!" yelled the big boy. The puppy barked in excitement and ran after Alec. Then the big boy began to run after him, too. "Oh dear," thought Alec, his heart beginning to beat fast. "What does that horrid big boy want? He may want to fight me. And that horrid dog of his is sure to bite me. I must run as fast as I can."

So there was Alec, running away as usual, his legs twinkling in and out so fast that they could hardly be seen. He puffed and he panted as he went, carrying the basket in his right hand.

The big boy raced after him, and the puppy-dog, too! "Hi! Hi! What are you running away for? Stop a minute! Come back! Do you hear me, come back!" shouted the big boy.

But Alec wasn't going to stop and he wasn't going to go back either. No – on he went, up the hill, into the lane, round the corner, over the stile, across the field, pant-pant-puff-puff, oh dear, oh dear, would he never be home!

The big boy followed him all the way, running on his long legs. The puppy almost caught him up—and then, oh, goodness me, just as Alec reached his own gate, the puppy ran in front of him, and tripped him up.

Alec fell to the ground with a crash. A jar of jam shot out of the basket and broke on the path. Alec's face bumped against the ground, and he got jam all over his nose and cheeks. What a sight he looked!

His mother came running out in dismay. "Alec, dear! Whatever's the matter? What were you running like that for? Oh dear, look at the jam!"

"Mother, mother, that horrid big boy has been after me all the way home!" panted poor Alec, tears running down his cheeks. "He chased me, and shouted after me, and set his dog on me, too. Mother, I've had an awful time—I've only just escaped him. He would have fought me, he would, really."

The big boy came running up, his face red and hot. Alec's mother turned to him.

"Why have you been chasing this little boy?" she said. "Why did you set your dog on him? That was very naughty of you. Look what you have made him do—upset my jar of jam and break it. Look at his poor face, all covered with jam."

"Well, I'm very sorry about that," said the big boy, "but it's not your jam, it's mine!"

"What do you mean?" said Alec's mother, in surprise.

"Well, we were both in the grocer's shop, having our baskets filled," said the big boy. "And suddenly this little fellow picked up my basket, instead of his own, and ran off at top speed with it! Of course, I yelled after him to come back. I wanted to give him his own basket, you see. But he simply would not come back! He ran on and on and on."

"And you had to run after him to get back your basket!" said Alec's mother. "And your puppy came with you, enjoying the excitement."

"Yes," said the big boy. "He wouldn't hurt anyone, my old rascal of a pup. He just came with me, that's all. I'm sorry your little boy fell down – but

really, if only he had stopped a minute instead of running away, everything would have been quite all right."

"He's always running away from things," said his mother, sadly.

"Perhaps he was meant to be a little girl, not a boy," said the big boy. "He looks more like a little girl than a boy, doesn't he? You expect little girls to run away."

"Well – I never ran away from anything when I was a little girl," said Alec's mother. "Never. Now, Alec – go and get some money from your money-box to pay for this jam."

"Oh, that's all right," said the big boy. "I can explain it to my mother. She'll understand. I don't want to take the little boy's money. I'm sorry for him."

"You're a nice boy," said Alec's mother. "I wish you lived near here so that you could sometimes play with Alec. You would do him good."

"Well, I do live near here," said the big boy. "I have come to stay with my aunt, next door but two. I don't know any other children here – so shall I come and play with Alec?"

"Come to tea today," said Alec's mother. "I don't know whether Alec will run away when he sees you coming in at the gate. He might do."

"I shan't," said Alec, who had been listening to all this with a very red face. "I want him to come to tea. He thinks I'm very silly, but I'm not. I'll show him!"

"Righto. Good for you!" said the big boy, with a laugh. "But mind – I'm going to bring my puppy."

"Well, if Alec runs away from either you or your puppy, you can have tea with me alone, and we'll have a fine time," said Alec's mother. "I've wanted a boy like you for a long time."

The big boy came to tea and his puppy, too. Alec didn't run away. He really had felt so silly and ashamed of himself that morning to think that he had run away with somebody else's basket, and had been scared of a nice boy and a jolly puppy-dog.

Now they are all good friends, and Alec is learning to be brave, and not run away. The big boy laughs at him and teases him, plays with him, and is very fond of him. So maybe some day Alec will be like you and never run away from anything at all! It's a stupid thing to do, isn't it?

The Train That Went to Fairyland

Once, when Fred was playing with his railway train in the garden, a very strange thing happened.

Fred had just wound up his engine, fastened the carriages to it, and sent them off on the lines, when he heard a small, high voice.

"That's it, look! That's what I was telling you about! This boy has got one!"

Fred looked round in surprise. At first he saw no one – then, standing by a daisy-plant, he saw a tiny fellow dressed in railway guard's uniform – but he had little wings poking out from the back of his coat! He was talking to another tiny fellow, who was dressed like a porter.

"Hallo!" said Fred in surprise. "Who are you and what do you want?"

"Listen," said the tiny guard. "will you lend us your train just for a little while – to go to Goblin Town and back? You see, the chief goblin is taking a train from Toadstool Town – and our engine has broken down. We can't get enough magic in time to mend it – and the chief goblin is getting awfully angry."

"Lend you my train?" said Fred, in the greatest astonishment and delight. "Of course I will – but you must promise me something first."

"What?" asked the little guard.

"You must make me small and let me drive the train," said Fred.

"All right. That's easy," said the guard. "But you won't have an accident, will you?"

"Of course not," said Fred. "I know how to drive my own train!"

"Shut your eyes and keep still a minute," said the guard. Fred did as he was told, and the little guard sang out a string of very queer words. And when Fred opened his eyes again, what a surprise for him! He was as small as the tiny guard and porter.

"This is fun!" said Fred, getting into the cab. "Come on. Will the engine run all right without lines, do you suppose?"

"Oh, we've got enough magic to make those as we go along," said the little guard – and at once some lines spread before them, running right down the garden to the hedge at the bottom.

"Well – off we go!" said Fred. "I suppose the engine has only got to follow the lines, and it will be all right!"

He pulled down the little handle that started the train, and off they went! The guard and the porter had climbed into the cab of the engine too, so it seemed rather crowded.

The lines spread before them in a most magical manner as the train ran over them – down the garden – through a hole in the hedge – and then, goodness me, down a dark rabbit-hole!

"Hallo, hallo!" said Fred in surprise. "Wherever are we going?"

"It's all right," said the little guard. "This will take us to Toadstool Town. We come up at the other side of the hill."

The engine ran through winding rabbit-holes, and once or twice met a rabbit who looked very scared indeed. Then it came up into the open air again, and there was Toadstool Town!

"I should have known it was without being told," said Fred, looking round him in delight as they passed tiny houses made out of the toadstools growing everywhere. "Hallo – we're running into a station!"

So they were. It was Toadstool Station. Standing on another line was the train belonging to the little guard. The engine-driver and stoker were trying their hardest to rub enough magic into the wheels to start it – but it just wouldn't go!

On the platform was a fat, important-looking goblin, stamping up and down.

"Never heard of such a thing!" he kept saying, in a loud and angry voice. "Never in my life! Keeping me waiting like this! Another minute and I'll turn the train into a caterpillar, and the driver and stoker into two leaves for it to feed on!"

"What a horrid fellow!" whispered Fred. The guard ran to the goblin and bowed low.

"Please, your Highness – we've got another train to take you home. Will you get in?"

"About time something was done!" said the goblin, crossly. "I never heard of such a thing in my life – keeping me waiting like this!"

He got into one of the carriages. He had to get in through the roof, because the doors were only pretend ones and wouldn't open. The little guard slid the roof open and then shut it again over the angry goblin.

TOADSTOOL T
TATION

"Start up the train again quickly!" he cried. So Fred pulled down the handle again and the little clockwork train set off to Goblin Town. It passed through many little stations with queer names, and the little fo'k waiting there stared in the greatest surprise to see such an unusual train.

Fred was as proud and pleased as could be! He drove that engine as if he had driven engines all his life. He wished and wished he could make it whistle. But it only had a pretend whistle.

Suddenly the train slowed down and stopped.

"Good gracious! What's the matter?" said the little guard, who was still in the engine cab with Fred. "Don't say your train is going to break down, too? The goblin certainly will turn us all into some-

thing unpleasant if it does!"

The goblin saw that the train had stopped. He slid back the roof of his carriage and popped his angry face out.

"What's the matter? Has this train broken down, too? I never heard of such a thing in my life!"

Fred had jumped down from the cab and had gone to turn the key that wound up the engine. It had run down – and no wonder, for it had come a long, long way! It was surprising that it hadn't needed winding up before.

The goblin stared in astonishment at the key in Fred's hand. He had never seen a key to wind up an engine before. He got crosser than ever.

"What are you getting down from the engine for? Surely you are not going to pick flowers or do a bit of shopping? Get back at once and set the train going."

But Fred had had enough of the cross goblin. He tapped him hard on the head with the key, and slid the roof back so that the goblin couldn't open it again.

"Now you be quiet," said Fred. "The pixies and elves may be frightened of you, but I'm not! Here I've come with my train to help you, and all you do is yell at me and be most impolite. I don't like you. I'll take you to Goblin Town with pleasure, and leave you there with even greater pleasure – but whilst we are on the way you will please keep quiet and behave yourself."

Well! The little guard and porter nearly fell out of the cab with horror and astonishment when they heard Fred speaking like that to the chief goblin! But Fred only grinned, and wound up the engine quickly.

There wasn't a sound from the goblin. Not a sound. He wasn't used to being spoken to like that. He thought Fred must be a great and mighty wizard to dare to speak so angrily to him. He was frightened. He sat in his roofed-in carriage and didn't say a word.

The train went on to Goblin Town and stopped. Fred got down, slid back the roof of the goblin's carriage and told him to get out.

The goblin climbed out quickly, looking quite scared.

"What do you say for being brought here in my train?" said Fred, catching hold of the goblin's arm tightly.

"Oh, th-th-thank you," stammered the goblin.

"I should think so!" said Fred. "I never heard of such a thing – not thanking anyone for a kindness. You go home and learn some manners, goblin."

"Yes – yes, I will, thank you, sir," said the chief goblin, and ran away as fast as ever he could. Everyone at the station stared in amazement.

"However did you dare to talk to him like that?" said the little guard in surprise. "Do you know, that is the first time in his life he has ever said 'Thank you'! What a wonderful boy you are!"

"Not at all," said Fred, getting back into the engine cab. "That's the only way to talk to rude people. Didn't you know? Now then – back home we go, to my own garden!"

And back home they went, past all the funny little stations to Toadstool Town, down into the rabbit burrows, and out into the field, through the hedge and up the garden, back to where they started from.

"Shut your eyes and we'll make you your own size again," said the little guard. In a trice Fred was very large indeed—and his train now looked very small to him!

"What would you like for a reward?" said the little guard. "Shall I give your train a real whistle, and real smoke in its funnel? Would you like that?"

"Rather!" said Fred. And from that very day his clockwork engine could whistle and smoke exactly like a real one. I do wish you could see it. It's really wonderful.

Dolly and Sue

"Hey, Dolly! Hey, Sue!" calls Fred, the farmer's son. "Get along there, now – we've a lot to do today!"

Dolly and Sue are two lovely farm horses. Dolly is the white one and Sue is the brown one. How hard they both work for the farmer and his son!

Their day begins at six o'clock in the morning when Fred comes along to the field where they have spent a peaceful night. They are ready for him, and they whinny and put their big velvety noses on his shoulder.

"We've work to do, my bonnies!" says Fred. "We must plough the Long Field and we must cart turnips and mangels to the sheep."

Dolly and Sue don't mind what they do. They like hard work. They like to feel the wind blowing their manes and the sun warming their backs. They love to hear Fred's friendly voice talking to them.

Here they are working hard with Fred. At twelve o'clock they will all have a rest and a meal. If Fred is a long way from his house he will sit down and open a packet of sandwiches in the shelter of a hedge. Dolly and Sue don't sit down. They wander about, pulling at the rich grass by the side of the meadow.

Sometimes they drink from the stream that runs beside the field. But as soon as Fred calls they trot back to him.

"Ready for work again?" he says, and they toss their big heads and swish their long tails. Of course they are ready for work—especially if it is for Fred.

In winter time they sleep in their fine stables at night, and then Fred goes there to fetch them in the mornings. It is dark on winter mornings, and sometimes he brings a lantern.

But winter or summer, Dolly and Sue are happy working with Fred, the farmer's son. Sometimes, when he is tired after a long day's work, Dolly gives a whinny in his ear. That means "Fred, get up on my back, and I'll carry you home!"

Then Fred mounts her and takes her and Sue to their stables to rest—and goes to his own little home on the hillside. "He's gone to his stable, Sue," says Dolly. "But he'll come for us again tomorrow."

Oh, Simple Simon!

Once little Simple Simon went to buy himself a fine big red balloon from the balloon woman in the market place. His mother had given him two pennies, and he meant to choose a good one.

He bought a beauty. You can see it, as red as can be, bobbing along in the air behind him. But, as he went along, his shoe-lace came undone. So Simon tied his balloon carefully to one of the iron railings nearby, and then did up his lace.

He undid the string from the railings and went on his way again. He didn't notice that he had undone the wrong string.

Mr. Barn the farmer had tied up his big goose there—and Simple Simon had undone the goose's string instead of the one belonging to his balloon! So there he goes, taking the goose behind him on the string, instead of his balloon!

The goose didn't like Simon, because he pulled so hard. Simon couldn't think why the balloon dragged behind. He pulled harder still at the string.

"Ss-ss-ss-ss!" hissed the angry goose.

"It's no good hissing at me, balloon," said

Simon, tugging at the string again, but not looking round. "You just come along!"

"Ss-ss-ss-SSSSS!" said the goose, and stood still. Simon turned round then. How he stared when he saw the big, hissing goose!

"Cackle, cackle, cackle!" said the goose, and tried to peck Simon with her beak. He dropped the string and ran for his life.

"Ma!" he yelled. "Ma! My balloon hisses and it's turned into a goose. MA!"

His mother came to the front gate in surprise. "Don't be silly, Simon," she said. "A balloon doesn't turn into a goose."

"Mine did!" said Simon. "You can see it did. Oh, Ma—what's happened?"

"Why, that's Farmer Barn's goose," said his mother, in surprise. "Dear me—how did you come to lead his old goose home? He will be cross!"

It wasn't long before Farmer Barn came round the corner to look for his goose. How cross he was with Simon!

"What do you mean by going off with my goose!" he roared. "Leaving me a silly red balloon instead! I'll spank you if you play tricks like that again!"

Simon went to get his balloon, feeling really very silly. But when he got to the railings, it had gone! A big wind had come and tugged so hard at the string that it had blown the balloon right away.

"Well, well—two geese and one balloon," said

Simon's mother. "And now there's only one goose left."

"Where's the one goose?" asked Simon, looking all round.

"Here!" said his mother, and she gave him a little push. "You're the goose that's left—and what a little goose you are, Simon, to be sure!"

Mr. No

Mr. No had a very good name. He said "No!" to so many things!

"Spare a penny to help to buy Mrs. Very-Poor a comfy chair," said Brownie Long-Beard.

"No," said Mr. No.

"Will you buy a ticket for the Pixies' Concert?" asked little Silver-Wings.

"No," said Mr. No.

"Do please spare a penny for old Mr. Tiptap whose house has been burnt down!" begged Dame Big-Feet.

"NO!" said Mr. No. "No, no, NO!"

"One of these days, Mr. No, somebody will put a spell on you to punish you for your meanness!" said Dame Big-Feet. But Mr. No only laughed.

Now one morning he went shopping with his big basket. He went to collect his magnificent new suit. He bought himself a fine hat with a feather in it. He spent fifty pence on a big chocolate cake, and ten pence on a bag of toffees. Then he bought himself a silver brooch with the letter N on it, to wear with his new suit.

He sat down on the wooden seat at the bus-stop. His basket was heavy, so he put it down. Other people came to wait, too. Dame Big-Feet was there, and she glared at Mr. No. "Anyone put a spell on you yet, for your meanness?" she asked. Mr. No didn't answer. He just glared back at her.

The bus came. Everyone picked up their baskets and got in. Mr. No pushed in first, of course, as he always did, no matter who was waiting for the bus.

He got home at last and put down his basket. "Now I'll have a toffee and cut myself a slice of cake – and then I'll try on my new suit and pin the brooch to the collar," he said. "And last of all I'll put on my grand feathered hat! How really magnificent I shall look!"

He looked inside the paper bag, meaning to take out a toffee. But dear me, how strange – there were no toffees, but just a stale old bone! "Queer!" said Mr. No, and opened the box to take out the big chocolate cake. But no chocolate cake was there – only just a few stale slices of bread!

Mr. No didn't like it. He began to feel most uncomfortable. What had happened?

"Oh dear – I hardly like to open the parcel my suit is in," said Mr. No. "There's something very queer about all this!"

And when he opened it, what a shock for him! Inside was a dirty old dress, torn and ragged. And would you believe it, instead of his magnificent hat, there was a dreadful old cap with a torn lining. And there was no silver brooch with N on, of

PIXIE
CONCERT

course, but instead there was a broken bead necklace. How Mr. No stared!

He sat down very suddenly. Somebody had put a spell on him for his meanness! Dame Big-Feet had always said it would happen, and now it had. What was more, it might go on happening if he went on being mean! Mr. No felt very worried indeed.

"I'll go straight and buy a cushion for Mrs. Very-Poor's chair," he said. "And I'll buy two tickets for the Pixies' Concert. And as for old Mr. Tiptap whose house has been burnt down, well – I'll take him my best carpet for the room that Dame Big-Feet is lending him!"

How surprised they all were to find Mr. No bringing these things to them! How they thanked him and praised him – and how warm and pleased he felt. Really, it was a very nice feeling to be kind and generous!

"Now perhaps that dirty old dress and cap will have changed back to my own new suit and feathered hat," he thought, hurrying home. "And the other things will have changed back, too."

But alas, they hadn't! "Never mind!" said Mr. No. "Perhaps if I keep on being kind and generous instead of mean the spell won't work again. I really couldn't bear it if all my nice things changed into nasty ones!"

Poor Mr. No! He didn't know that Mr. Blinks, the old brownie from Far-Off Village, had picked up the wrong basket, and had left his own for Mr.

No. Both baskets were exactly alike, you see. How astonished Mr. Blinks was when he found such a wonderful set of things in his basket!

"Dear, dear – there's the scraps for the birds changed into a cake – and the dog's bone changed into toffees – and look at this wonderful suit and hat in place of the old things I was taking to the jumble sale!" said Mr. Blinks, in delight. "And what a dear little silver brooch, instead of that old bead necklace I was going to have mended for my wife, Nellie. N on it, too, for Nellie!"

He really thought that some nice person had put a good spell into his basket and had changed all his old things into beautiful new ones. He was very happy indeed.

As for Mr. No, the shock had been very good for him indeed. He isn't called by that name now. Can you guess what it has been changed to? Well, you're right – he's called Mr. YES!

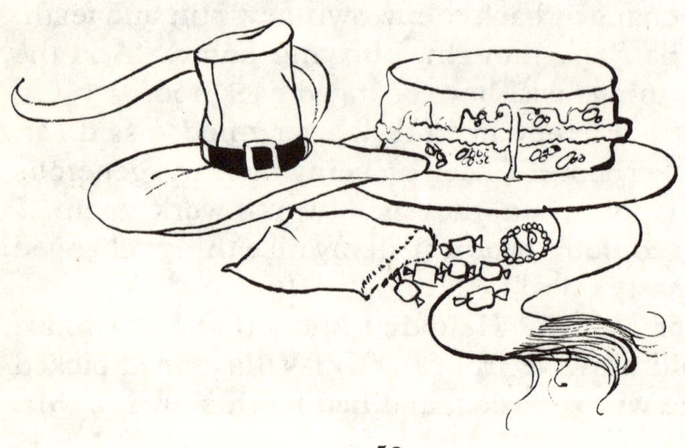

Don't Tell Anyone

Once the teddy bear found a little piece of chocolate on the floor. One of the children had dropped it and hadn't noticed.

"Oooh! Chocolate!" said the bear to himself, in delight. He looked round to see if anyone was about. No, nobody was. Good!

The bear picked up the bit of chocolate and wondered where to hide it. "I'll put it somewhere where I can go and lick it when I want to," he thought. So where do you suppose he put it?

He stuck it in the funnel of the wooden engine! The engine wasn't very big and the bit of chocolate fitted nicely into the funnel. The bear gave it a lick before he left it.

He simply couldn't help telling the little clockwork mouse. "There's a nice bit of chocolate stuck in the engine-funnel," he said. "Don't tell anyone!"

Well, of course, the first thing the mouse did was to go and have a good lick at the chocolate. The golliwog saw him and was most surprised.

"Why are you licking the engine-funnel?" he said.

"Sh! There's a bit of chocolate there," said the clockwork mouse. "Don't tell anyone!"

The golliwog was astonished. As soon as he had a chance he went to the engine, climbed up behind the funnel and had a very fine lick at the bit of chocolate there. Then he went to tell the toy dog.

"Don't tell anyone—but there's a bit of chocolate down the engine-funnel," he whispered. The toy dog was delighted. Chocolate! Well, he would go and have a lick when nobody was looking.

So off he went as soon as he could. Now, being a dog, he had a very fine tongue for licking, and he licked and he licked and he licked. Soon he had licked so much that there was only the tiniest bit of chocolate left, and that slid down to the very bottom of the funnel.

"You look very pleased with yourself, toy dog," said the teddy bear, meeting him on the hearth rug.

"Well, I am," said the toy dog. "I know a secret. Don't tell anyone! There's a tiny bit of chocolate down the engine-funnel!"

"But that's MY secret!" wailed the bear, and he rushed over to the engine. Alas, he couldn't even see the bit of chocolate, let alone lick it with his little pink tongue.

He was very angry. "I'll spank the person who told my secret!" he cried. "Toy dog, who told you?"

"The golliwog," said the dog. So the bear rushed

across to the golliwog and shouted at him.

"How did you know my secret? Who told you?"

"The clockwork mouse told me," said the golliwog.

"Oh, the bad fellow!" shouted the angry teddy bear. "Who told him, I wonder? I'll spank him, I really will spank him!"

The clockwork mouse poked his head out of the brick-box, where he was hiding.

"Well, go and spank yourself," he said. "You told me about the bit of chocolate. You gave away your own secret. Ha ha! You aren't very clever, are you, teddy bear? You had a lovely bit of chocolate to lick—and now it's all gone!"

Poor teddy! He still goes and looks down the engine-funnel every night, but nobody can reach the tiny bit of chocolate that is left. What a pity he gave his own secret away!